The Shoalhaven

SOUTH COAST NEW SOUTH WALES

Photography and Text by
BRIAN and SUE KENDRICK

A Lightstorm Publication

Published by Lightstorm Publishing ©
Distributed by Lightstorm Photography
P.O. Box 1167, Nowra NSW 2541
Ph: (044) 46 6007 Fax: (044) 46 6008

Hanimex Pty Ltd
108 Old Pittwater Rd
Brookvale NSW 2100
Ph: (02) 938 0400

All the photographs in this book were taken on
Fuji Velvia and Fuji Provia 100 transparency film.
Their outstanding sharpness and beautiful colour
made them our films of choice.

*Title Page: Perched atop the vertical cliffs of Beecroft
Peninsula, Point Perpendicular Lighthouse marks the
northern entrance to Jervis Bay.*

*Right: The delightful harbour of Ulladulla, home of the
region's largest commercial fishing fleet.*

*Overleaf, clockwise from top left: The ketch Seander at
Greenwell Point jetty; officers in training, HMAS
Creswell; hand-feeding a crimson rosella at Greenpatch,
Jervis Bay National Park; overlooking Morton National
Park from one of the many 4WD tracks which traverse the
area; Drum Major of the Shoalhaven City Pipe Band;
boardriders at Mollymook Beach; a young angler with a
prize catch of yellowfin tuna; tame kangaroos at Pebbly
Beach in Murramarang National Park.*

C O N T E N T S

INTRODUCTION

The Shoalhaven district is located on the New South Wales coast, 160 kilometres south of Sydney. Stretching from the picturesque town of Berry in the north to Durras in the south, its eastern border is fringed by pristine beaches of white sand interspersed with dramatic sandstone cliffs and rocky headlands, while the mountains of the Morton and Budawang National Parks stand sentinel over its western extremity.

The original inhabitants of the region were Aborigines from the Wodi Wodi, Dharumba and Wandandian tribes, who have lived in the Shoalhaven region for more than 20,000 years. The first European to sight the area was Captain Cook, who named Pigeon House Mountain in April 1770, but it wasn't until 1797 that George Bass gave the area its name. He discovered the mouth of a river, well guarded by shoals, which he named 'Shoals Haven'. Although he was actually describing the mouth of the Crookhaven River the name was subsequently applied to the main river and later to the district. Apart from itinerant settlement by cedar cutters and whalers the area remained largely uninhabited by Europeans until Alexander Berry and Edward Wollstonecraft took up a lease of 10,000 acres on the northern bank of the Shoalhaven River in 1822. These days, the Shoalhaven region is home to more than 73,000 people and is one of the fastest growing localities in New South Wales.

An area of enormous geographic diversity, the district offers visitors an opportunity to experience a wide range of activities. Anglers, surfers, sailboard riders and swimmers have over 100 beaches to choose from, including Hyams beach, which boasts the whitest sand in the world. Rock climbers come from near and far to tackle the near vertical cliffs of Point Perpendicular, while scuba divers enjoy the clear water and unique marine life of Jervis Bay. Yachting enthusiasts revel in the region's spectacular sailing while bushwalkers and canoeists find their challenge in the mountains and rivers of Morton and Budawang National Parks. The region's natural treasures are protected in over 300,000 hectares of parks, state forests and reserves.

The towns of the Shoalhaven offer a variety of temptations. Berry, town of trees, is famous for its antique and specialty shops, while Kangaroo Valley boasts numerous beautiful craft shops. Nowra, with a population of more than 23,000 is the administrative and

▶ *Map by courtesy of J.K. Craigie* ©

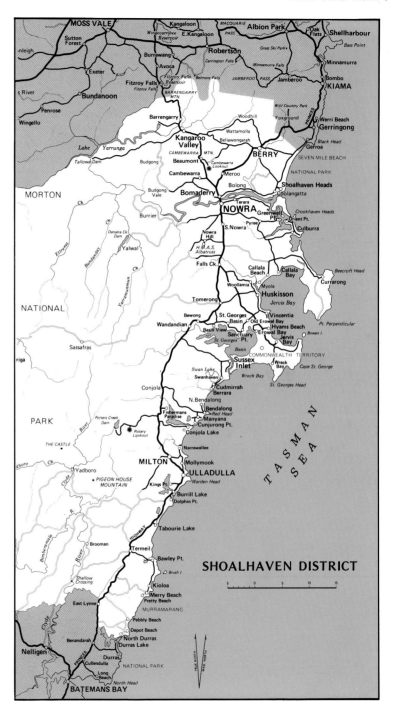

SHOALHAVEN DISTRICT

commercial centre of the region and provides all services. The delightful village of Huskisson is the stepping off point for scuba diving, penguin and dolphin watch tours, while further south the Ulladulla, Mollymook area is a popular centre for golf, surfing, fishing and diving. Throughout the region are numerous small towns and villages, each offering their own special appeal.

Dairy farming and forest industries have been important to the region since the early days of European settlement, but these days commercial fishing also plays a major role. The region has an active manufacturing sector and Shoalhaven Paper, Shoalhaven Starches and Australian Co-operative Foods are three of the largest employers. The Royal Australian Navy has had a presence in the district since 1915 when the R.A.N. College was constructed at Jervis Bay. During the Second World War the British navy established a Fleet Air Arm base near Nowra Hill, 7 kilometres south west of Nowra, which was transferred to the R.A.N. in 1948 and commissioned as HMAS *Albatross*.

In the same year the councils of Nowra, Numbaa, Shoalhaven, Broughton Vale, Broughton Creek, Bomaderry, Ulladulla, Berry, Cambewarra and Clyde amalgamated to form the Shire of Shoalhaven. Today, tourism is the major industry in a region whose scenic beauty attracts more than two million visitors each year.

The Crookhaven River at sunset, viewed from Crookhaven Heads.

H I S T O R Y

ABORIGINAL HISTORY

Twenty thousand years ago, the most recent ice age was coming to an end and the Shoalhaven coastline was approximately 20 kilometres further east than it is today. At that time, the region was already inhabited by Aborigines, but as the ice melted the sea level rose slowly, burying much of the archaeological evidence of habitation beneath metres of sea and sand. The sea reached its present level approximately 6,000 years ago and from this time numerous archaeological sites survive, which provide evidence of the Aboriginal lifestyle. Excavation has revealed the shells of edible shellfish, bones of fish, the remains of a variety of mammals, charcoal, hearthstones, bone and shell artifacts.

Seafood formed the basis of the Aboriginal diet and shell middens provide evidence of the types of food which were eaten. Until 1,000 years ago shellfish were collected and fish were caught in the mouths of estuaries and close to the shore, but more recently bark canoes were used to fish further offshore. Bowen Island offered good hunting, where penguins and mutton birds were captured and bones from these animals are found both on the island and in shell middens on the mainland. Small marsupials from the forests fringing the coast formed a regular part of the diet, while larger sea mammals such as seals were also eaten occasionally. Although plant foods would undoubtedly have formed a major part of the diet, little evidence of this remains. With such a bountiful and varied supply of food and a temperate climate it is thought that the indigenous people would have enjoyed a good lifestyle.

Tools were manufactured from bone, stone or shell. Flaked stone artifacts such as cutting and scraping tools, spear barbs and points have been excavated from campsite locations throughout the Shoalhaven. Due to the soft nature of the local stone, stone for axe-heads was traded from considerable distances. Axe grinding grooves, where the heads were ground to a smooth cutting edge, can be seen on sandstone outcrops such as the stream bed above Mary Bay. Although evidence of rock art is not extensive in the region, paintings have been found in rock shelters on the Beecroft Peninsula.

Aboriginal names are prominent as place names throughout the region. Coolangatta means splendid view, Culburra means sand, Myola is a place of crabs and Nowra is the word for black cockatoo. Ulladulla is a corruption of the Aboriginal word Woolahderra which means safe harbour and Cambewarra is a combination of two words, camba meaning fire and warra meaning mountain, probably because of the Illawarra flame trees which used to grow there. Captain Cook bestowed the name Pigeon House Mountain on the remarkable outcrop of stone which dominates the skyline in the south of the region, but the Aboriginal people know it as as Dithol, which means woman's breast.

The first encounter the Aborigines had with Europeans were merely two races sighting each other from a distance. It wasn't until 1797 that direct contact first occurred, when survivors from a ship wreck at Point Hicks in Victoria were making their way northward. As they travelled through the lands of many different tribes they were received in a friendly manner where it was perceived they were passing through, and with hostility if they were viewed as permanent invaders.

In the latter years of the eighteenth century the indigenous people would have witnessed regular visits from whalers and cedar cutters, but it wasn't until Alexander Berry took up a grant of 10,000 acres on the Shoalhaven River in 1822 that settlement by Europeans commenced in earnest and the traditional lifestyle of the Aboriginal people was threatened. Once the country was stocked with sheep and cattle, many of the edible plants disappeared and the Aborigines were forced away from their traditional hunting grounds. Contact with

Upper Right: One of several murals painted on the walls of the South Coast Aboriginal Centre. This painting by artists Jason Mcleod, Reggie Ryan and Arthur Wellington took three months to complete and depicts the sighting of the First Fleet.

▶ *A painting on bark by Jeff Timbery illustrates the generations of his family and their traditional lifestyle. The abundant food supply of the area is depicted which included turtle, fish, birds, platypus and crab. The serpent was the dreamtime figure responsible for the formation of rivers, valleys and mountains.*

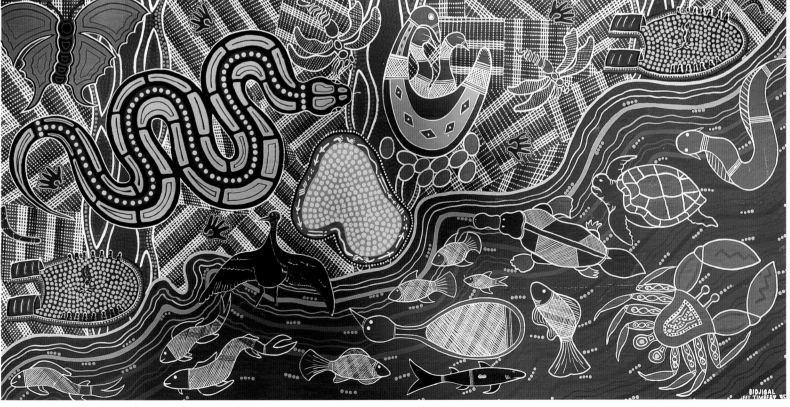

Europeans also brought new diseases such as smallpox, influenza, measles and syphilis. During the early decades of the 19th century, some traditional food gathering practices were maintained, but by the 1830's the former population had been decimated by the combined effects of disease and the removal of land and those who remained were relocated to reserves such as Roseby Park at Orient Point and Bilong at Myola.

By 1914 small groups of Aboriginal fisherman had settled at Wreck Bay, south of Jervis Bay, and in 1952 the area was gazetted as an Aboriginal Reserve. The Wreck Bay Community were granted land rights over an area of 403 hectares in 1986 and today the community numbers about 50 families, most descended from or related to the first settlers at Wreck Bay. In June 1995 the Federal Government offered the title of the Jervis Bay National Park to the Wreck Bay Aboriginal Community upon the condition that it was leased back to the Australian Nature Conservation Agency for a period of 99 years.

▶ *A view over Summercloud Bay toward the Aboriginal lands of Wreck Bay. Groups of Aboriginal fishermen moved to Wreck Bay in 1914, but it wasn't until 1986 that they were granted title to the land*

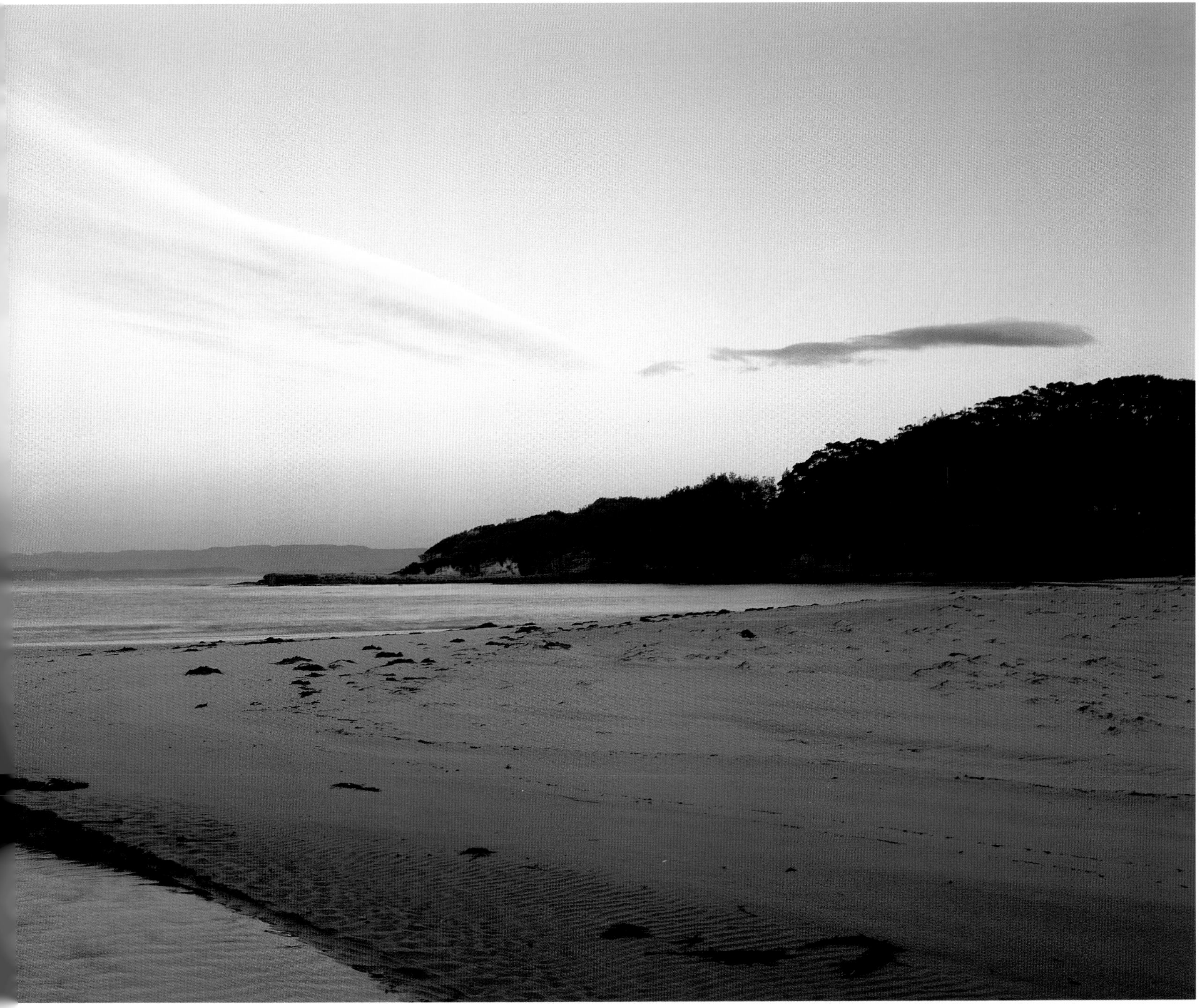

EXPLORATION AND SETTLEMENT

The first sighting of the Shoalhaven region by Europeans most probably took place as Captain Cook and his crew sailed northward along the New South Wales coast in the HMAS *Endeavour* during April 1770. In his log Cook described 'a remarkable peaked hill which resembled a square dove house with a dome on top', which he called Pigeon House Mountain. Further north, he noted in his log the entrance to Jervis Bay, but sailed on without giving it a name. His journal reveals that he was taking advantage of favourable winds and to 'beat up' would have taken more time than he was prepared to spare. Had he decided to investigate he would have discovered the deepest natural harbour in Australia.

Twenty one years later Lieutenant Bowen named the bay Port Jervis, (in honour of his former naval commander Sir John Jervis), when he sailed into its protected waters in the *Atlantic* seeking shelter from adverse winds. Although Bowen and his crew did not go ashore he noted in his log 'the wisdom of training young naval officers in seamanship here'.

Whilst others visited the region in the ensuing years, it wasn't until 1797 that George Bass gave the region its name on his epic journey south in an open whaleboat. He discovered the mouth of a river, well guarded by sandy shoals, which he named 'Shoals Haven'. Although he was actually describing the mouth of the Crookhaven River, the name was soon applied to the main river and eventually to the region. Bass was unimpressed with the country he saw, describing it as generally barren, although he did note that the area to the south of the bay may prove suitable for cattle.

The first European settlement was of an itinerant nature; whalers worked out of the safe haven of Jervis Bay and timber cutters felled red cedar in the forests. But it wasn't until 1811 that any serious exploration occurred when surveyor George Evans came ashore near the present town of Huskisson. He journeyed along Currambene Creek, crossed the Shoalhaven River west of Nowra then climbed Mount Cambewarra. When Surveyor General John Oxley visited the area 8 years later he described what he saw as 'miserable, sterile country' and noted that he could see no place where 'even a cabbage might be planted with a prospect of success'.

Despite such discouraging reports, Alexander Berry recognised the potential of the region for farming after exploration of the area in early 1822. Six months later he and his partner Edward Wollstonecraft took up a grant of 10,000 acres (4,047 hectares) on the Shoalhaven River in exchange for the maintenance of 100 convicts. Permanent settlement of the region then commenced in earnest.

Because of the shoals which made the mouth of the Shoalhaven River dangerous, Berry set the convicts to work cutting a canal across the narrow sand spit which separated it from the Crookhaven River. The canal was completed in just twelve days and it remains the route of egress to the sea for the Shoalhaven River. Berry chose to build his homestead at the base of the hill known by Aboriginals as 'Collungatta' and soon a self-supporting village grew in its shadow. The new community was entirely dependent upon the river for transport of goods to and from the port of Sydney.

In the south of the region settlement commenced when Reverend Thomas Kendall received a grant of 1280 acres (518 hectares) just north of the present township of Milton, which he took up in 1828. He called the property 'Kendall Dale' and ran cattle and felled cedar with ticket-of-leave men (paroled convicts). His grandson, the celebrated poet Henry Kendall, was born on the estate. The surrounding area was soon taken up and became known as 'The Settlement', which the first postmaster later changed to Milton in honour of the great English poet. The early residents of Milton used the natural harbour seven kilometres further south, which they called Boat Harbour but the name was later changed to Ulladulla, thought to be a corruption of the Aboriginal word 'Woollahderra', which means safe harbour.

The mainstays of the regional economy in the early years of settlement were dairy farming and timber cutting, both of which remain important industries today. Tobacco, potatoes, maize and other crops were also produced, principally for the Sydney market. In the early years wheat was grown but rust, a fungal disease, eventually affected the crop and the industry collapsed. When wool prices began to rise in the 1840's, a track

◄ *Pigeon House Mountain, sighted by Captain Cook in April 1770, was the first landmark in the region to be given a European name. The Aboriginal people know the mountain as Dithol, which means woman's breast.*

called 'The Wool Road' was cut across the mountains from Braidwood to Jervis Bay and wool and tallow became important exports.

By the early 1850's Terara, on the south bank of the Shoalhaven River, had become the commercial, social and cultural centre for the people south of the river. A series of disastrous floods in 1860, 1870 and 1874 completely destroyed the town and forced the relocation to Nowra, which was well sited on higher ground. Construction of a bridge over the Shoalhaven River in 1881 to replace the punts and ferries confirmed Nowra's status as the new commercial centre of the district.

Following Federation in 1901, and the naming of Canberra as the national capital in 1911, Jervis Bay was selected as a port for the new capital. An area of land on the southern side of the bay along with Bowen Island and part of the bay itself, was transferred from New South Wales to the Commonwealth. Within these boundaries the newly formed Royal Australian Navy made recommendation for the creation of a Naval College, which was completed in 1915. Thus, Lieutenant Bowen's vision in 1791, of a training centre for naval officers, was realised.

Ambitious residential developments were also planned for the shores of Jervis Bay in the light of the Government's decision to build the federal port there, but when a planned rail link with Canberra failed to eventuate these plans did not materialise.

Despite this, the Shoalhaven region has continued to prosper throughout the twentieth century, and today it is one of the fastest growing areas of New South Wales. While the historic industries of dairy farming and forestry remain central to the economy, recognition of the region's natural beauty means that tourism is now the most important industry.

◀ *The Great Hall, formerly the community hall and church for Alexander Berry's Coolangatta Estate, is now a restaurant at the Coolangatta Historic Village.*

▶ *A map detailing development plans for the Jervis Bay area after the Government announced plans to develop its federal port there. Displaying the unmistakable influence of Walter Burley Griffin, the broad, curved avenues reminiscent of Canberra never eventuated.*

Overleaf: Historic Hampden Bridge, which spans the Kangaroo River in the township of Kangaroo Valley, was completed in May 1898. The wooden suspension bridge with its castellated sandstone pylons is the only bridge of its type remaining in Australia. Just five days after its completion the old bridge was washed away by floodwaters.

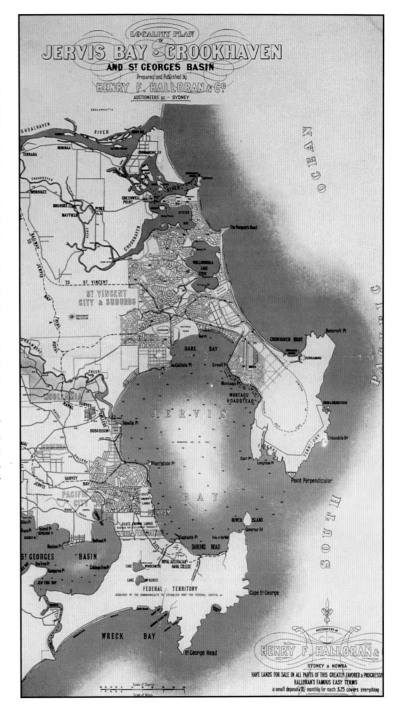

Previous Page: Inside the Coach House Restaurant of the Hotel Berry. In 1863 Alexander Berry constructed what was then called the Broughton Creek Kangaroo Inn for his workers. The Coach House Restaurant, located in what was originally the kitchen outhouse of the inn, specialises in the use of local produce, including fresh seafood and game. Its culinary excellence was rewarded in 1994 when it received the Australian Hotels Association award for best NSW country restaurant.

◄　*Point Perpendicular Lighthouse, which stands at the northern entrance of Jervis Bay, was built in 1899 after years of complaint from sailors regarding the Cape St George Lighthouse a few kilometres to the south. Constructed from Conjola sandstone, the lighthouse and its three adjacent cottages are classified by the National Trust.*

▼　*The Cape St George Lighthouse, constructed in 1860, was apparently built in the wrong location and could not be seen by ships approaching from the south! After construction of the new light at Point Perpendicular, the original lighthouse became a navigational hazard during daylight hours so was used by the navy as a target for bombing practise and is now a crumbling ruin.*

►　*The gymnasium building, with its striking clocktower, dominates the parade ground at HMAS Creswell, Jervis Bay. When the college took its first cadets in 1915 it fulfilled Lieutenant Bowen's prophesy of 1791 that Jervis Bay would be an ideal location for the training of young naval officers. The clock is thought to be the only one on land to ring the watch.*

◀ *The Ulladulla Lighthouse, built in Wollongong and erected on the pier at Ulladulla in 1873, was subsequently moved to nearby Warden Head in 1889. One of only two cast iron lighthouses in Australia, it is unusual in still having its original optical apparatus intact and in use.*

▼ *The Thompson's Bakery building in Milton is now a private residence but was once a bank. It has also been used as a doctor's surgery and hospital, when beds were frequently placed around the verandah.*

▶ *Hackett's Restaurant, on the highway in Milton, was originally a general store. Constructed from blocks of granite circa 1842, the building features cedar doors, windows and stairwell.*

Overleaf: A favourite launching place for hang gliders, Cambewarra Lookout offers a magnificent view over Nowra toward Jervis Bay. The canal connecting the Shoalhaven and Crookhaven Rivers, cut by Alexander Berry's convict labour, can be seen in the middle distance.

T O W N S

A large part of the Shoalhaven's appeal derives from the number of small towns and villages found within its borders. From Kangaroo Valley in the north, with its craft and specialty shops, to the historic village of Milton in the south, the towns of the Shoalhaven offer a glimpse of the past, or an opportunity to enjoy one of the many leisure activities for which the region is famous.

Nowra

In the early years of European settlement people were slow to settle in Nowra and the religious, social and commercial life of the district was centred at Terara, a few kilometres downstream.

Although Nowra township was declared in 1852, it wasn't until a disastrous flood struck Terara in 1860 that Nowra began to assume dominance as the centre of the district. Terara suffered again in the floods of 1870, thereby consolidating Nowra's growing position of importance in the region. The building of the bridge over the Shoalhaven River in 1881 adjacent to the town assured its future prosperity.

Nowra's first hotel opened in the 1850's, its first store in 1861, the first official school in 1862 and by 1880 all four of the major denominations had built churches in the town.

In the early years of this century the Royal Australian Navy built its training college at Jervis Bay, thereby starting a long association between the navy and the town.

With a population of more than 23,000 Nowra is now the administrative and commercial centre of the Shoalhaven region and the focus of an active manufacturing sector.

Berry

Known as the town of trees, Berry is the northernmost town in the Shoalhaven region. Originally named Broughton Creek, it was changed in 1890 to honour the Berry family, first European settlers of the region.

The town prospered in the 1880's and many of the beautiful historic buildings which lend such character to the Berry streetscape date from this period. The Post and Telegraph Office, opened in 1886, is now a delightful coffee shop while the adjacent English Scottish and Australian Bank building houses the Berry Museum.

These days Berry is famous for its antique and craft shops as well as its historic charm. On the first Sunday of each month the Berry market offers an enticing variety of local art and craft in an atmosphere of country charm.

Above right: Outdoor cafés are a feature of the Berry streetscape.

▶ *Bellissima fine handcrafts, one of Berry's many tempting specialty shops.*

◀ *The Shoalhaven River Bridge was constructed in 1881 and the new bridge in the background, 99 years later. Since 1860 Nowra has experienced 19 floods when water levels have exceeded 5 metres under the bridge.*

Kangaroo Valley

When explorer George Evans first set eyes on Kangaroo Valley in 1812 he saw 'A view no painter could beautify'. Nestled between Cambewarra and Barrengarry mountains, Kangaroo Valley township is the centre of a rich farming district. Weathering of the volcanic Kangaroo Mountain and Broughton Head yielded lush alluvial floodplains, watered by the Kangaroo River. The valley's beauty has also attracted artists and craftsmen, and visitors are treated to a wonderful choice of local handcrafts from the many specialty shops of the valley.

The first European settlement was itinerant in nature; in 1820 Cornelius O'Brien and Captain Richard Brooks both sent cattle over the range to graze on the floodplains of the Kangaroo River and provided huts for their men in the valley. The cedar cutters followed in the 1830's and cedar cutting continued in the valley until the free selectors cleared the last remaining stands in the 1860's.

In 1840 Henry Osborne was granted 2,560 acres in the centre of the valley at Barrengarry and the growing settlement became known for a time as the Private Township of Osborne. Dairy farming was soon established as the valley's principal industry and by the early 1890's there were four factories processing milk in the district. Gradual improvements in transport and refrigeration had forced their closure by 1925, but dairy farming remains a major industry in the valley today.

Greenwell Point

In 1829 Greenwell Point became the Shoalhaven's first port when Alexander Berry constructed a wharf there for the large ships calling from Sydney and Melbourne.

By 1888, commercial fishing and oyster growing were established and these industries remain important to the economy of the town today. The Greenwell Point population is now approximately 1200, many of whom are involved in the fishing or tourism industries. Visitors to the town are attracted by its reputation for excellent fishing in the river, which yields catches of flathead. bream and mullet, while others like to sample the fresh oysters and famous fish and chips available on the waterfront.

Culburra, Orient Point and Currarong

Best known as holiday destinations, these three towns are famous for their beaches and their access to excellent ocean, river and rock fishing sites. Each summer the population of the towns swell as tourists arrive to enjoy the sun, sand and surf while warm evenings and weekends see Nowra residents flock to the surf beach at Culburra.

Above right: Valley Wood Crafts specialise in the manufacture of wooden rocking horses, which are not only popular in Australia but exported all over the world.
◀ *The Friendly Inn, Kangaroo Valley's only pub, is a famous watering hole not only for motorbike riders who enjoy the winding roads leading into the valley, but for all lovers of fine food in a country pub atmosphere.*
▶ *Fishing the Crookhaven River*

The towns of Jervis Bay

Spread around the shoreline of Jervis Bay are several towns and villages, all popular with holiday makers for their safe, sheltered beaches which are ideally suited to swimming and sailing.

The centre of tourist activities on the bay is Huskisson, with several operators catering for scuba divers keen to experience the diverse marine life and exceptionally clear waters of the bay. The town is also the stepping off point for dolphin and penguin watch tours.

Situated where Currambene Creek enters Jervis Bay, Huskisson has always been a town with a strong association with the sea. In 1861 George Dent started building boats at the mouth of the creek and ship building soon became the town's major industry. One ship built by Dent was the Sydney harbour ferry, the Lady Denman, which was returned to Huskisson after decommissioning in 1979 to become the focal point of the Lady Denman Heritage Complex. Also within the complex is the Lady Denman Maritime Museum and Laddie Timbery's famous Bidjigal Aboriginal Arts and Crafts centre.

Sussex Inlet, St Georges Basin and Sanctuary Point

Sussex Inlet lies on a stretch of river joining St Georges Basin with the sea. The first European settler in the region was Jacob Ellmoos, a Danish migrant who established a farm on the northern side of the river in 1880. His family were commercial fishermen but they soon became famous for their guest house, Christian's Minde, which opened in 1896.

Known as the island township, Sussex Inlet is located on the south bank of the river and today numbers more than 2000 permanent residents. In the summer this number increases dramatically as holiday makers flock to the area to take advantage of the wide variety of water sports, while the Family Fishing competition in the winter school holidays attracts anglers from near and far.

The idyllic setting of the St Georges Basin and Sanctuary Point townships have made them the fastest growing towns in the Shoalhaven region in recent years. The protected waters of the basin lend themselves to sailing, swimming and water skiing and the numerous boat ramps in the area give easy access to Sussex Inlet and the ocean.

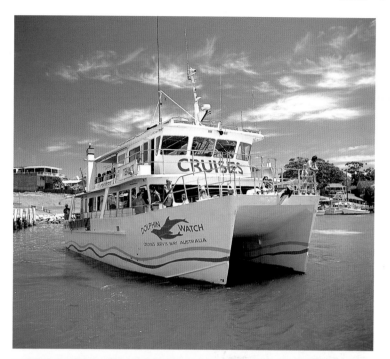

Above right: Dolphin watch tours depart from Huskisson, offering tourists the opportunity to view these intelligent mammals in their natural environment. Other tours visit Bowen Island at dusk to see Fairy Penguins returning to their nests.

◀ *The characteristic red and green hire boats at Sussex Inlet are popular with anglers keen to take advantage of excellent fishing in the river and St Georges Basin. Christian's Minde is visible in the background.*

▶ *The town of Hyams Beach, on the shores of Jervis Bay, is said to have the whitest sand in the world.*

Milton

Reverend Thomas Kendall was the first European to settle in the south of the region after taking up a grant of land near the present township of Milton in 1828. On his property 'Kendall Dale' he ran cattle and felled cedar until his untimely death in 1932. He was aboard the schooner *Brisbane* when it was wrecked taking a cargo of cedar and cheese to Sydney. The fifth generation of Kendall's family still work the original holding in Milton.

Milton's contemporary appeal owes much to its past; the many beautifully preserved historic buildings lend character and charm to this delightful town.

Mollymook

Located 6 kilometres southeast of Milton, the township of Mollymook is famous for its excellent surfing beaches and championship golf course. The earliest settlers in the area were Henry and Ellen Mitchell who called their farm Molly Moke, probably after the Mollymawk, a specie of Albatross which visited the coastline in spring.

While Mollymook has been a popular leisure centre with locals since the early years of this century it is only in the last two decades that the town has grown into the leading tourist resort that it is today.

Ulladulla

Originally known as Boat Harbour, then as Wasp Harbour, Ulladulla was important in the early days of European settlement as the port for the township of Milton and the surrounding farming districts. It wasn't until well into this century that Ulladulla's population exceeded that of Milton and it became the centre of commerce in the south of the region. Today, the combined population in the Milton, Ulladulla area is more than 10,000.

Professional fishing was started in the 1930's by three Italian families and today Ulladulla is home to the region's largest commercial fishing fleet. The annual 'Blessing of the Fleet' festival on Easter Sunday is a colourful spectacle which follows this Italian custom.

Burrill Lake and Kioloa

These southern Shoalhaven towns were timber towns in the early days of their settlement and at one time the mill at Kioloa was reputed to be the largest in the southern hemisphere, employing more than 70 men.

Campers began visiting the area in the 1920's to enjoy the beautiful, unspoilt beaches and excellent fishing. In addition to these traditional leisure activities, today's holiday makers also enjoy windsurfing, water skiing and sailing on Burrill Lake. The spotted gum forest, lovely beaches and tame kangaroos of Pebbly and Depot Beaches are just a short drive south of Kioloa.

Above right: Surfers ready to tackle the waves at Mollymook. The golf clubhouse in the background offers a breathtaking view along the beach.
◄ *The delightful seaside town of Ulladulla, with its picturesque harbour, is the commercial centre for the south of the Shoalhaven.*
▶ *Body-boarding at one of the many excellent surfing beaches in the region's south.*

P A R K S

Within its total area of 466,250 hectares the Shoalhaven region has more than 300,000 hectares of parks, state forests and reserves. Seven Mile Beach, Jervis Bay, Murramarang, Morton and Budawang National Parks preserve a variety of important ecosystems while many smaller nature reserves exist throughout the region to protect specific plant and animal habitats. These parks and reserves also offer an enormous variety of recreational activities including fishing, surfing, bushwalking, rock climbing, birdwatching and canoeing.

SEVEN MILE BEACH NATIONAL PARK

Located on the coastline between Gerroa and Shoalhaven Heads, the 730 hectare Seven Mile Beach National Park preserves an important coastal dune system. The shifting foredunes are stabilised by hardy, salt-resistant spinifex while the permanently established dunes feature thickets of coastal tea-tree and wattle. The park provides habitat protection for a variety of birds, including honeyeaters, thornbills and white-throated tree creepers. The long expanse of Seven Mile Beach offers excellent fishing and surfing, while walking trails allow exploration of the forest area behind the dunes. Day visitors will enjoy the resident kookaburra population while taking advantage of the excellent picnic facilities in the park.

JERVIS BAY NATIONAL PARKS

Over the years the pristine beauty of Jervis Bay has been threatened on many occasions. A steel mill was proposed for Currambene Creek in 1969, a nuclear power station was mooted for Murrays Beach in the 1970's and most recently, it was recommended that the East Coast Armaments Complex be relocated to Cabbage Tree Point on the Beecroft Peninsula. None of these development plans have come to fruition and Jervis Bay remains a place of outstanding natural beauty.

Large sections of Jervis Bay are now protected in parks and reserves. In April 1994 the State Government announced its decision to establish the New South Wales Jervis Bay National Park. The northern part of Beecroft

Previous Page: The long sweep of Seven Mile Beach viewed from the Kingsford Smith Memorial Lookout at Gerroa.

Above Right: A rock shelter at Abraham's Bosom on the Beecroft Peninsula. Excavation of this site has revealed that the shelter was used by Aborigines a number of times each year to cook, make and repair tools.

▶   *The Rainbow Lorikeet, Trichoglossus haematodus, is common throughout the Shoalhaven region. A blossom feeder, it harvests nectar and pollen from many plants including eucalypts, paperbarks and banksias.*

◀   *Looking along the spectacular coastal cliffs of the Beecroft Peninsula toward 'Old Man's Hat'. Land-based game fishing from rock platforms at the base of these cliffs yields catches of tuna, yellowtail kingfish and the occasional black marlin.*

Peninsula is included in the park, along with large sections of land adjacent to Jervis Bay not already taken up by residential developments.

At the southern end of Jervis Bay, much of the land annexed from NSW in 1911 to provide a port for the national capital is now protected within the Jervis Bay National Park, administered by the Australian Nature Conservation Agency. Included in this park are large sections of the Bherwerre Peninsula, Bowen Island and the southern waters of the bay. The balance of Jervis Bay's marine environment is protected in the Jervis Bay Marine Reserve.

Lying on the overlap of temperate and southern climatic zones, the Jervis Bay National Parks contain an astonishing number of plant and animal species. A wide variety of habitats has added to this diversity; dune systems, beaches, coastal cliffs, heaths, forests, swamps and estuarine areas are all present within the park.

Within these diverse habitats a range of recreational activities are enjoyed by visitors to the park; Bherwerre, Cave and Steamers beaches offer excellent surfing while the calm waters and dazzling white sands of the bayside beaches are popular with families. The outstanding opportunities for land-based game fishing from the rocky headlands of Beecroft Peninsula attract anglers to the area, while bushwalkers are well provided for with numerous walking trails. The Green Patch area, with its resident population of tame crimson rosellas, gallahs, king parrots and other birds, is the park's major attraction.

Aboriginal people have lived in the Jervis Bay area for more than 20,000 years and the park protects sites containing archaeological evidence of their traditional lifestyle. Some of the descendants of the original inhabitants of the area now live at Wreck Bay. In June 1995 the Federal Government offered the title to the lands of the Jervis Bay National Park to the Wreck Bay Aboriginal Community, conditional upon it being leased back to the Australian Nature Conservation Agency for a period of 99 years.

Jervis Bay Botanic Gardens

Located within Jervis Bay National Park, the Botanic Gardens are an annexe of the Australian National Botanic Gardens in Canberra. Established in 1951, the gardens provide frost-free growing conditions for many plants unsuited to Canberra's climate. Covering an area of 80 hectares, the gardens have an emphasis on the flora of the coastal regions of southeast Australia and contain both natural and cultivated areas. Pleasant walks criss-cross the gardens and pass through natural bushland of scribbly gum and heath to the lush greenery of Rainforest Gully.

◄ *An aerial view along Captains Beach to the R.A.N. College, HMAS Creswell. The track in the foreground leads to the popular Iluka picnic area in the Jervis Bay National Park.*

▶ *The exceptional clarity of the water in Jervis Bay is due to an absence of major rivers draining into the bay. The dazzling white sands of the bay's fringing beaches are said to be the whitest in the world.*

◄ *'Hole in the Wall', an eroded sandstone outcrop on the Bherwerre Peninsula, Jervis Bay National Park.*

▶ *Rainforest Gully, in the heart of the Jervis Bay Botanic Gardens.*

▼ *Banksia ericifolia, which blooms prolifically throughout winter and spring, is common on the sandstone plateaus of Jervis Bay National Park. The nectar of its flowers is an important food source for many birds and insects.*

Jervis Bay Marine Reserve

Although the exceptional features of Jervis Bay's marine environment were recognised as worthy of protection as long ago as 1975, it wasn't until 1995 that the Jervis Bay Marine Reserve was finally declared. Located at a mixing point of warm northern waters, cooler temperate waters and cold southern waters, Jervis Bay supports an enormous diversity of marine species including more than 200 species of fish and 200 species of invertebrates. A wide variety of habitats adds to this diversity and includes mangrove areas, intertidal zones, subtidal rocky reefs, caves, drop-offs, a variety of soft-bottom habitats and the most extensive sea-grass meadows in NSW. With no major rivers draining into the bay, its exceptionally clear waters support some species at greater depths than elsewhere.

The long beaches of white sand, crystal clear water and prolific marine life attracts scuba divers, snorkelers, anglers, swimmers, surfers and sightseers to the Jervis Bay Marine Reserve. The bay also hosts visiting whales on their annual migration and boasts four pods of semi-resident dolphins totalling more than 80 individuals. Dolphin watch trips and boat tours to the penguin rookeries on Bowen Island are some of the new ecotourism-based activities which are becoming increasingly popular.

The Jervis Bay Marine Reserve aims to protect the exceptional marine heritage of the bay, whilst still allowing for recreational and commercial activities to continue. To this end, particularly vulnerable areas such as sea grass meadows have been identified and are protected within sanctuary zones, while less sensitive areas will be managed on the principles of ecological sustainability.

MURRAMARANG NATIONAL PARK

Declared a National Park in 1973, Murramarang is the southernmost park in the Shoalhaven region and covers more than 1700 hectares of coastal land south of Kioloa. Wasp, Grasshopper, O'Hara and Dawsons Islands are also included in the park, sections of which extend beyond the southern border of the Shoalhaven.

The predominant plant community in the park is spotted gum with an understorey of ancient burrawang palms, while rainforest pockets occur in the sheltered gullies around Durras Mountain. These forests are home to many animals, including the eastern grey kangaroo, swamp wallaby and red-necked wallaby. Finches, honeyeaters and a variety of sea birds are frequently sighted, and the large numbers of tame crimson rosellas and king parrots in the park delight visitors with their antics.

Above Right: Hand-feeding a crimson rosella.

◄ *The resident population of tame eastern grey kangaroos at Pebbly Beach. Grasshopper Island, visible in the background, is also included in Murramarang National Park.*

▶ *The Coral Tree, Erythrina x sykesii, was planted extensively in the early years of settlement as hedgerows and its brilliant red flowers remain a feature of the Shoalhaven landscape.*

Murramarang's biggest attraction is undoubtedly its resident population of eastern grey kangaroos, which are frequently seen on the vegetated dunes at Depot and Pebbly Beach. Accustomed to humans, these gentle animals can be observed at close quarters as they crop the grass on the dunes and have even been seen taking to the water on hot summer days.

Swimmers, surfers and anglers have many beaches and headlands to choose from within Murramarang, while walkers who climb Durras Mountain are rewarded by spectacular views of the coastline and adjacent ranges.

MORTON NATIONAL PARK

By far the largest park in the Shoalhaven region, Morton National Park covers an area of 162,000 hectares of escarpment from Bundanoon in the north to Pigeon House Mountain in the south. Characterised by sandstone plateaus and deep ravines, the park is a thickly forested wilderness dissected by fast flowing streams.

A great variation in the landform within the park provides habitats for a range of animals including kangaroos, wallabies, snakes, lizards and a variety of birdlife. Numerous rare and some endangered species are found within Morton, such as brush-tailed rock wallabies, ground parrots and tiger quolls. Rare plant species include Pigeon House ash, Budawang ash and Ettrema mallee.

The northern section of Morton protects a long stretch of the Shoalhaven River, both upstream and downstream from Tallowa Dam, where picnic and camping facilities are provided. In the south of the park Pigeon House Mountain dominates the landscape and is a popular destination for rock climbers attracted by the steep cliffs of the escarpment. For bushwalkers the three hour hike to the summit offers magnificent views to the coast and south into adjoining Budawang National Park.

BUDAWANG NATIONAL PARK

Adjoining the southern end of Morton National Park, this 16,000 hectare wilderness is inaccessible by vehicle. The open forests of the western slopes are dominated by peppermint gum while silvertop ash grow on the ridges and steep hillsides. The park also contains some of the most southerly patches of subtropical rainforest. Experienced bushwalkers enjoy the challenging walks in Budawang National Park.

◀ *Located within Morton National Park, Pigeon House Mountain dominates the skyline in the south of the region. The three hour hike to its 721 metre summit affords sweeping views to the coast.*

▶ *An enjoyable drive on a well graded gravel road from Tomerong leads through Yerriyong State Forest into the Morton National Park, where Tianjara Falls plunge to the valley below.*

Overleaf: The tranquil waters, sandy beaches and dramatic sandstone cliffs of the Shoalhaven River attract water skiers and swimmers. Artist Arthur Boyd has been greatly inspired by these subjects since his first visit in 1971.

BUNDANON TRUST

In March 1993, artist Arthur Boyd and his wife Yvonne made an extraordinary gift to the people of Australia. With an estimated value of more than $12 million, their gift included the properties of Bundanon, Riversdale and Earie Park, along with an enormous collection of artwork, photographs and letters, spanning four generations of the Boyd family. Located on the Shoalhaven River near Nowra, the combined Bundanon properties total more than 1,000 hectares and in 1993 a public company, the Bundanon Trust, was established by the Government to manage and develop this important natural and cultural heritage.

The Bundanon Trust aims to promote enjoyment of the arts by making the Bundanon properties a 'living arts centre', for the exhibition and creation of art. By preserving the natural and cultural heritage of Bundanon, the Trust hopes to encourage an appreciation of the Australian landscape.

Arthur and Yvonne Boyd fell in love with the Shoalhaven when they visited the Bundanon property in 1971. At that time it was owned by Sydney art dealer Frank McDonald and his partners Sandra and Tony McGrath. The Boyds became interested in purchasing a property in the area, but they were in London in 1973 when Riversdale, the property adjoining Bundanon, was placed on the market. McDonald sent them photographs and the sale was completed by mail! Several years later the Boyds purchased Bundanon.

The historic Bundanon homestead was built in 1866 for Dr Kenneth McKenzie, a Scot who had come to Australia thirty years earlier. The colonial mansion is constructed of sandstone quarried nearby and features extensive use of cedar cut from the property. Boyd's timber studio, purpose built in the 1970's, is separated from the house by a delightful cottage garden filled with sculptures by members of the Boyd family.

The Bundanon property is open to the public on one Sunday of each month, when visitors are treated to tours through the house, studio and grounds of this magnificent estate.

◀ *The historic Bundanon homestead, built in 1866 from sandstone and cedar taken from the property, is listed on the Register of the National Estate. Arthur and Yvonne Boyd live at Bundanon as artists in residence whenever they are in Australia.*

▶ *'The Swimmer', a bronze statue by Arthur's brother Guy Boyd, in the gardens of Bundanon.*

◀ *An incomplete painting stands on the easel in Boyd's studio at Bundanon. Illuminated by skylights and large windows, the studio is separated from the house by beautiful gardens. From the time of his first visit to the region in 1971, Boyd commenced painting Shoalhaven subjects almost exclusively; nudes in the bush, landscapes, (sometimes incorporating mythological or religious figures), and more recently his series of bathers and waterskiers.*

▼ *A kaleidoscope of oils on Arthur Boyd's palette in the Bundanon studio.*

▶ *Arthur and Yvonne Boyd in the grounds of Bundanon. These days the Boyds divide their time between Bundanon and a cottage in Suffolk, England.*

▼ *Arthur Boyd was named Australian of the Year in 1995 in recognition of 'his contribution to Australian art and the generosity and vision of the Bundanon and many other gifts to the Australian people.'*

Overleaf: The beautiful Riversdale property, overlooking the Shoalhaven River, is the focus of an 'artist in residence' program and the trust has plans for an education centre there.

THE ROYAL AUSTRALIAN NAVY

HMAS *CRESWELL*

The Royal Australian Navy has played an important role in the history of the Shoalhaven region, dating back to the establishment of an officers' training college in 1913. Parliament decided to locate the college at Jervis Bay as part of its plan to develop a federal port there. During the construction phase training was based at Osborne House Geelong, but moved to Jervis Bay on completion of the buildings in 1915.

Between the years of 1916 and 1930 the college produced graduates who formed the backbone of naval officers serving both ashore and afloat. The harsh economic climate of the depression saw a restriction in the number of cadet entrants and in 1930 the college was forced to move to the Flinders Naval Depot in Victoria. The site was then used as a resort until 1958, when the college returned to Jervis Bay and was commissioned as HMAS *Creswell*.

In the early days, cadet entrants were as young as 13 years of age and their four year course finished with their matriculation. These days, only professional naval training is conducted; all tertiary education is undertaken at the Australian Defence Force Academy in Canberra. Professional training at the college includes courses for qualified men and women joining the RAN, and are designed to impart the service skills and knowledge required of all officers. In addition, skills training for junior officers is conducted by the RAN Staff Training School, while the RAN School of Survivability and Ships' Safety is the lead school for training personnel in nuclear, biological, chemical defence and damage control throughout the navy.

The HMAS *Creswell* base has a delightful location, built atop low cliffs which overlook the waters of Jervis Bay to Point Perpendicular and Bowen Island. In recognition of its historic significance and its special value for present and future generations, the entire area of the naval college has been placed on the register of the Australian Heritage Commission.

Visitors will appreciate the many fine historic buildings as well as the tame wildlife, which includes a resident population of more than 100 kangaroos. The college is open to the public on weekends and public holidays.

◀ *Sub-Lieutenant Romina Sciberras and Lieutenant Michael Elsley in the grounds of HMAS Creswell.*

▶ *Personnel from the New Entry Officers Course practise for their passing out parade.*

The delightful HMAS Creswell base on the shores of Jervis Bay. The first intake of 87 cadets in 1915 realised a prophesy made by Lieutenant Bowen in 1791, when he noted in his ship's log the wisdom of training young naval officers in seamanship here. During the depression years the college was forced to relocate to Flinders Naval Depot, but returned to its former home in 1958 when it was commissioned HMAS Creswell in honour of Vice Admiral Sir William Creswell, KCMG, KBE. Today, the tradition continues with the training of professional naval officers at the base.

▼ *The commissioning bell of the HMAS Creswell, located adjacent to the parade ground.*

HMAS ALBATROSS

Soon after WWII was declared in 1939, a decision was made to build an airfield at Nowra Hill, 7 kilometres south west of Nowra, and in May 1942 the Royal Australian Air Force occupied the base. The RAAF were soon followed by the US Army Air Corps and the Netherlands East Indies Air Force. When the British Admiralty directed some of its naval forces to the South West Pacific in 1944 it required shore based facilities for the Royal Navy and its Fleet Air Arm. The RAAF Base at Nowra was considered an ideal location because of its proximity to Jervis Bay, which was large enough to accommodate the entire British Fleet. The Royal Navy's Fleet Air Arm began operations at Nowra in October 1944 but in 1946 the base reverted to RAAF control.

In July 1947 the Commonwealth Defence Council approved the formation of a Fleet Air Arm, to be controlled and operated by the Royal Australian Navy, with shore facilities based at Nowra. HMAS *Albatross* was comissioned on 31st August 1948. Since then the base has continued to grow, with ground support facilities expanding to service the increasingly sophisticated equipment.

These days, *Albatross* is the largest employer in the Shoalhaven with more than 1000 service and 300 civilian personnel. Service members and their families total more than 3000, and their contribution to the economy of the region is enormous. This contribution is not merely an economic one: over the years, bush fire and flood relief assistance have been provided as well as searches and rescues of bushwalkers and fishermen.

THE AUSTRALIAN NAVAL AVIATION MUSEUM

The Australian Naval Aviation Museum was established at HMAS *Albatross* in 1974. Situated at the northern end of the base, the museum's historic collection documents Australia's involvement in naval aviation. Aircraft equipment, weaponry and models of aircraft and carriers are complemented by photographic displays. The Family Air Days, held 6 times each year, are a major attraction in the region and feature demonstration flights by vintage and contemporary aircraft along with a parachute display by the 'Red Berets', members of the army's parachute training school.

Above Right: 723 Squadron pilot Sub-Lieutenant Kimble Taylor at the the controls of a Squirrel helicopter

◀ *A demonstration by one of the 817 Squadron's Sea King helicopters on Family Air Day.*

▶ *Inside the Australian Naval Aviation Museum at HMAS Albatross.*

I N D U S T R I E S

From the earliest days of settlement the principal industries of the Shoalhaven region were timber and dairying, and both industries remain central to the economy of the region today. An active manufacturing sector now complements these traditional industries, boosting the local economy by an estimated $300 million dollars annually and providing more than 3000 jobs.

The region also boasts many small and cottage industries which contribute significantly to the appeal of the area. Wine making commenced in 1976 when the first vines were planted at Jasper Valley, apiarists take advantage of the large reserves of native forest and craft industries add colour to the region.

Now recognised as the most popular tourist destination in New South Wales, the region's thriving tourism industry provides more than 3,700 jobs and boosts the local economy by a further $305 million per year, making it the region's largest industry.

Fishing Industry

Commercial fishing in the Shoalhaven region is centred at Ulladulla and Greenwell Point, with some smaller boats operating from Jervis Bay. The fishing industry at Ulladulla was started by three Italian families in the 1930's and the first trawler started operating from Greenwell Point in 1945. These days, trawlers from both ports fish the ocean bed for table fish such as flathead, john dory, red fish, ocean perch and ling, live-baiters from Greenwell Point target kingfish, tuna and bonito while long liners from Ulladulla catch yellowfin, big-eye and southern blue-fin tuna for the lucrative sashimi market.

Almost all fish from Greenwell Point and part of the Ulladulla catch is transported to the Sydney market, with the balance exported directly to Japan for sale as sashimi. Fish caught in the morning leaves Ulladulla the same afternoon and is flown from Sydney to Japan overnight. The next morning it is sold in the Japanese fish markets!

Oyster farming has been established in the Shoalhaven and Crookhaven Rivers for more than 100 years but it wasn't until approximately 35 years ago that the industry began to expand to the size it is today. There are now more than 30 farmers supplying Shoalhaven, Wollongong and Sydney markets with the famous Sydney Rock Oyster.

Previous Page: Low tide at Greenwell Point reveals the extensive oyster leases of the Crookhaven estuary.

Above Right: Kevin Gray, skipper of the Anne-Marie, with a catch of red fish.

▶ *World champion oyster shucker Jim Wild in his new shop at the Shoalhaven River Bridge.*

◀ *Part of the commercial fishing fleet at Ulladulla Harbour.*

Dairy Farming

Alexander Berry took up a grant of 10,000 acres (4,047 hectares) on the Shoalhaven River in January 1822 and on August 22nd of the same year the first draft of 93 cattle were driven into the region by Hamilton Hume. In the early years the Shoalhaven was used as a breeding ground for young stock but by 1850 dairying was established as the chief industry of the district.

Dairying remains an important industry for the Shoalhaven and the herds of Fresians grazing on the rich pasture of the coastal fringe are a characteristic of the regional landscape. The emphasis of dairy farming today is on production of quality milk and income is based on the protein, butterfat and bacteriological purity of the product, not simply the volume. Today's cows produce almost twice the milk of their predecessors of twenty years ago thanks to selective breeding, improved pasture and genetic engineering. Some farmers are now using computers to analyse the output of individual cows to increase their productivity even further.

Australian Co-operative Foods

Located on Bolong Road, Bomaderry, Australian Co-operative Foods receives milk from as far afield as Albion Park and Moruya for the production of milk products. Employing more than 100 people the factory supplies an enormous market bounded by Helensburgh, Cambelltown, Picton, Goulburn and Tuross Head.

Factory production includes whole milk and modified milks such a Shape, Lite White and Skim Milk, flavoured milks, cream, rich Burra Creek cream and Dynamite children's milk for schools. Modified sweetened condensed milk products are exported to Asian markets and are sold in bulk packs to Australian confectionary manufacturers.

Shoalhaven Starches

Located on Bolong Road adjacent to Australian Co-operative Foods, Shoalhaven Starches are part of the Manildra Group. The permanent workforce of more than 130 is complemented by contract labour to produce starch, gluten, glucose, fructose and ethanol.

The company is the largest manufacturer of glucose and the only manufacturer of fructose in Australia. While fructose is used as a general sweetener, glucose is supplied to brewers, jam makers, confectionary and ice cream manufacturers. Seventy percent of the company's production of starch is used in paper manufacture with the balance taken up for use in confectionary and baking. A valuable by-product of starch maufacture is ethanol, which is used in the production of methylated spirits, inks, dyes, cosmetics and pharmaceuticals. A $30 million expansion program is currently underway to produce fuel grade ethanol for use as a component of petrol. Producing a cleaner fuel, this important environmental initiative has been supported by a government subsidy.

Above Right: The Australian Co-operative Foods Factory at Bomaderry
▶ *Herds of Fresian cows are characteristic of the Shoalhaven landscape.*
◀ *Columns of the distillation plant at Shoalhaven Starches which are used in the production of ethanol.*

Forest Industries

The cedar forests of the Shoalhaven region attracted the first pioneers to the area and provided the mainstay of the local economy in the early years of permanent settlement. The Shoalhaven River provided an easy means of transporting the timber to Sydney and by January 1824, less than two years after taking up a grant of land in the region, Alexander Berry had more than 628,000 feet of cedar ready for shipment. Timber getters were quick to realise the importance of other trees and iron bark was soon being cut for use as railway sleepers and bridge decking, while turpentine was used for wharf pylons due to its natural resistance to marine borer.

Cedar is now rare, but these days forest reserves of more than 60,000 hectares yield native timbers such as spotted gum, blackbutt, iron bark, turpentine, scribbly gum, bloodwood, stringybark and bangalay, and are managed on a sustainable yield basis. The climate and soils of the region are largely unsuitable for plantation pine and only small pockets exist south of Ulladulla. The timber is milled locally and used in the Shoalhaven, Wollongong and Sydney markets. Since the 1960's the region has also been an important supplier of timber to the mining industry, for use as pit props.

The forestry industry is estimated to provide 180 jobs and contributes $5-7 million annually to the regional economy.

Shoalhaven paper

The Shoalhaven Paper Mill was commissioned in 1956 after two British paper companies, Wiggins Teape and William Nash, selected the site on Bolong Road, Bomaderry, because of its suitable water supply, access to rail transport, reliable supply of labour and proximity to Port Kembla for shipping.

Shoalhaven Paper began recycling paper in 1966 and is now the largest manufacturer of fine recycled papers and speciality paper products in Australia. The mill makes more than 600 grades of special papers, including the Optix range of coloured papers, Centurion parchment and Superfine prestige office stationery.

Today the mill employs more than 450 people and injects a total of $25 million annually into the local economy.

Above right: An apiarist tends his hives in the Currambene State Forest. The prolific flowers of the spotted gum are favoured by bee-keepers, as they provide a regular flow of quality honey.

◀ *An extensive network of access trails within the State Forests lead to camping and picnic areas, historical mining sites and areas of scenic beauty.*

▶ *Richard King and John Pick tend the King Proteas at their King Pick protea farm near Sussex Inlet; one of a growing number of innovative industries in the Shoalhaven.*

PHOTOGRAPHIC INFORMATION

The photographs in this book were taken using Art Panorama, Mamiya RZ67 and Canon EOS1 cameras, utilising a range of lenses. Filters were used occasionally to improve the quality of the images: a polarising filter controlled reflected light thereby improving colour saturation, a graduated filter was used when required to control the sky, an 81C filter was used in heavy shade for added warmth.

Fuji professional transparency film was used exclusively in this publication. The rich colour saturation and high resolution of Velvia made it our film of choice for landscape work, while Provia 100D, with excellent contrast and fine grain, was used for other subjects. For the aerial work, Provia 100 was push processed to yield an effective film speed of 200 ISO, yet the film still retained excellent sharpness and colour balance.

ALSO BY THE SAME AUTHORS....

AUSTRALIA BENEATH THE SOUTHERN CROSS

Sue and Brian Kendrick travelled Australia for eighteen months to collect the stunning photographs for their bestselling book *Australia Beneath the Southern Cross*. Using large format cameras, their photographs capture in fine detail the beauty and diversity of the Australian landscape. From the temperate rainforests of Tasmania to the deserts of central Australia, from the rugged gorges of the Kimberley to Queensland's Cape York Peninsula, they travelled more than 55,000 kilometres, and shot in excess of 7000 photographs. Avoiding cities and towns they journeyed into some of the most remote and isolated regions of the continent, into the **real** outback.

Take advantage of the special readers' price of $30.00 and join the thousands who have already experienced the splendour of this ancient continent, celebrated in *Australia Beneath the Southern Cross*. (180 pages full colour, hard back)

YELLOW WATERS ● KAKADU ● NT ● AUSTRALIA
Photography BRIAN KENDRICK

004

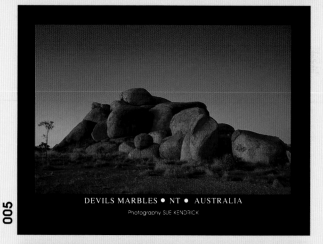

DEVILS MARBLES ● NT ● AUSTRALIA
Photography SUE KENDRICK

005

TWELVE APOSTLES●PT CAMPBELL NATIONAL PARK●VICTORIA●AUSTRALIA
Photography SUE KENDRICK

006

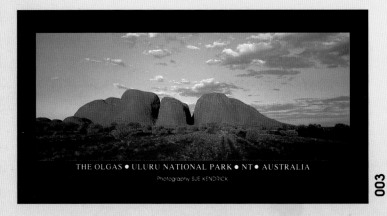

AUSTRALIA BENEATH THE SOUTHERN CROSS
ULURU STAR TRACE
Photography SUE and BRIAN KENDRICK
001

RIVERSLEIGH ● QUEENSLAND ● AUSTRALIA
Photography BRIAN KENDRICK
002

THE OLGAS ● ULURU NATIONAL PARK ● NT ● AUSTRALIA
Photography SUE KENDRICK
003

POSTER COLLECTION

From the famous landmarks of Uluru and the Twelve Apostles to the remote wilderness of Kakadu, this magnificent collection captures the essence of the Australian landscape. Printed on art paper, these beautiful reproductions are available framed, unframed or laminated and will make a stunning addition to your home or office.

Our framing service offers the choice of black or silver aluminium moulding with clear perspex, and is delivered to your door by courier.

Post to: Lightstorm Photography Pty Ltd P.O. Box 1167 Nowra NSW 2541
Australia Phone orders: (044) 466 007/Fax orders: (044) 466 008

QTY	DESCRIPTION		CODE	PRICE	TOTAL
	ULURU STAR TRACE	960mm x 500mm	001	10.00	
	RIVERSLEIGH	960mm x 500mm	002	20.00	
	OLGAS	960mm x 500mm	003	20.00	
	YELLOW WATERS	960mm x 500mm	004	20.00	
	DEVILS MARBLES	800mm x 600mm	005	20.00	
	TWELVE APOSTLES	800mm x 600mm	006	20.00	
	FRAMING IF REQUIRED	Black Silver		60.00	
	POSTER LAMINATION		PL	24.00	
	AUSTRALIA BENEATH THE SOUTHERN CROSS		BOOK	30.00	

Plus Postage **Australia** $5 Poster/Book   **Overseas** $10
$15 Framed **Posters Only**

I enclose my cheque/money order made payable to **TOTAL $**
Lightstorm Photography Pty Ltd

or debit my ☐ VISA   ☐ MASTERCARD   ☐ BANKCARD   ☐ AMEX

Card No. ☐☐☐☐☐☐☐☐☐☐☐☐☐☐☐☐☐☐

Expiry date: _____/_____

GUARANTEE If you are not satisfied with your purchase please return the order in good condition within 14 days and your full purchase price will be refunded.
Please use a photocopy of this page when placing your order.

Name _____
Address _____
_____ Postcode _____
Ph: _____ Fax: _____
Signature: _____

First Published 1995
© Copyright: Photographs and text Brian and Sue Kendrick 1995
Designed by Anne Esposito
Printed by Dai Nippon

National Library of Australia Cataloguing-in-Publication data
Kendrick, Brian
The Shoalhaven, south coast New South Wales

ISBN 0 646 24521 X

1. Shoalhaven (N.S.W.) - Pictorial works.
2. Shoalhaven (N.S.W.) - Description and travel
3. Shoalhaven (N.S.W.) - History
I. Kendrick, Sue. II. Title.
994.47

Many thanks to:
John Craigie for permission to reproduce the map on page 7
and Warren Halloran for permission to reproduce the map on page 17

and to individuals from the following organisations who have helped with this publication:
Australian Co-operative Foods: Australian Naval Aviation Museum;
Australian Nature Conservation Agency; The Bundanon Trust;
HMAS *Creswell*; HMAS *Albatross*; New South Wales Fisheries;
Shoalhaven Paper; Shoalhaven Starches; Shoalhaven Tourism
South Coast Aboriginal Cultural Centre; State Forests;
and the many others who have so freely given their time.